WHY DEACONS?

THE TEACHING OF POPE JOHN PAUL II

Introduced by Michael Evans

CTS Publications

*First published 1995 by the
Incorporated Catholic Truth Society
192 Vauxhall Bridge Road
London SW1V 1PD*

© *1995 The Incorporated Catholic Truth Society*

ISBN 0 85183 943 6

CONTENTS

Introduction — p.4

The teaching of Pope John Paul II — p.20

Selected official and liturgical texts — p.35

Notes — p.40

INTRODUCTION

The *Catechism of the Catholic Church* (n.1571) says of deacons:

> Since the Second Vatican Council the Latin Church has restored the diaconate 'as a proper and permanent rank of the hierarchy', while the Churches of the East had always maintained it. This permanent diaconate, which can be conferred on married men, constitutes an important enrichment for the Church's mission.

The diaconate was an important ministry in the early Church, but went into decline in the Middle Ages, becoming almost exclusively a step on the way to priesthood. The Council of Trent, 'burning with desire to restore the ancient usage', intended the restoration of the diaconate as a permanent ministry, but we had to wait until the Second Vatican Council and the decisions of Pope Paul VI for this restoration to be implemented. Now many parishes have grown accustomed to the ministry of a deacon. In 1994 there were 11,175 deacons in the USA, and more than 325 in England and Wales. Increasingly the diaconate is indeed being recognised as an 'important enrichment' for the life and mission of Christ's Church.

No one today is more warmly supportive of the permanent diaconate that Pope John Paul II, as can be seen from his 1987 talk to U.S. deacons and their wives in Detroit and his three General Audience addresses on the diaconate in October 1993. These texts are the central content of this booklet. Again and again the Pope highlights the importance of the diaconate. He cites the important witness of St Ignatius of Antioch as one who 'underscores the greatness of the deacon's ministry', and sees the restoration of this ministry as flowing from the fact that, 'on the basis of ancient teaching, the awareness of the diaconate's importance for the Church became greater and greater in theological and pastoral circles'.[1] To the U.S. deacons the Pope expressed his joy and sense of encouragement:

> It is a special joy for me to meet with you because you represent a great and visible sign of the working of the Holy Spirit in the wake of the Second Vatican Council, which provided for the restoration of the permanent diaconate in the Church. The wisdom of that provision is evident in your presence in such numbers today and in the fruitfulness of your ministries. With the whole Church, I give thanks to God for the call you have received and for your generous response. For the majority of you who are married, this response has been made possible by the love and support and collaboration of your wives. It is a great encouragement to know that in the United

States over the past two decades almost eight thousand permanent deacons have been ordained for the service of the Gospel.

The U.S. Bishops' Committee on the Permanent Diaconate has provided a number of excellent publications on this developing ministry, as have individual American Bishops.[2] Quite a few books have been published on the diaconate recently, all stressing its importance. These include James Barnett, *The Diaconate – a full and equal order* (Seabury Press, New York 1981); Edward Echlin, *The Deacon in the Church – past and future* (Alba House, New York 1971); Christine Hall (ed.), *The Deacon's Ministry* (Gracewing, Leominster 1991); Patrick McCaslin and Michael Lawler, *Sacrament of Service* (Paulist Press, New York 1986); Ormonde Plater, *Many Servants – an introduction to deacons* (Cowley Publications, Boston 1991) and Lynn Shermann, *The Deacon in the Church* (Alba House, New York 1991). All references to these authors in this article are to the works mentioned above.

In July 1994 Archbishop Crescenzio Sepe, secretary of the Congregation for the Clergy in Rome, gave an address to the National Catholic Diaconate Conference in the USA, entitled 'Diaconate: a great and visible sign of the work of the Holy Spirit'. The Congregation is currently directing much of its attention to deacons. A Plenary Session in October 1995 is being dedicated to questions about the diaconate, leading to the eventual publication of a document on the ministry and life of permanent deacons.[3]

So why is so much importance being given to the diaconate? Why do we have a growing number of deacons? And why *should* we? One thing we clearly need is a sound theology of the diaconate. As is often the case, deep reflection follows from lived experience, and we can expect a richer understanding of this ministry to develop as the permanent diaconate becomes more established and accepted. It is a sobering thought that the answer to the often put question 'What can a deacon do that a layperson cannot do?' is a blunt 'Nothing!' As with all ordained ministry, the first question should not be 'What can a deacon *do*?' but rather 'What *is* a deacon?'

An exalted office

Whatever people's doubts and hesitations, the diaconate is a *major* order in the Church, 'an exalted office' (St Hippolytus, *Apostolic Tradition*, 9). It is an integral part of the sacrament of orders, and in the end it is not specifically 'diaconal' functions but the fundamental Catholic notion of sacrament which is the key to answering our question 'Why deacons?' Without a true sense of sacramentality, the diaconate has little to offer which cannot be found elsewhere.

A sacrament of Jesus Christ

St Ignatius of Antioch (c. AD 100) reminds us that the bishop images the Father, presbyters image the apostles, and deacons ('especially dear to me', he says) image Jesus Christ. What should our attitude be towards deacons? Ignatius tells us: 'Let everyone respect the deacon as they would Jesus Christ' (*Trallians*, 2); 'Give your deacons the same reverence that you would to a command of God' (*Smyrna*, 8). The third century Syrian Document *Didascalia Apostolorum* develops this teaching: 'The bishop sits in the place of God almighty, but the deacon stands in the place of Christ, and you must love him' (2.26).

Pope Pius XII in 1947 taught that deacons as well as bishops and priests receive the sacrament of orders by the laying-on of hands (*Sacramentum Ordinis*). The Second Vatican Council spoke of deacons as 'strengthened by sacramental grace' (*Lumen Gentium*, 29; cf *Ad Gentes*, 16).

Pope Paul VI summed up the purpose and meaning of restoring the permanent diaconate in his letter *Ad Pascendum* in 1972. This ministry is to be *'a driving force for the Church's service'*, and the deacon is *'a sign or sacrament of the Lord Jesus Christ himself'*. Pope John Paul II affirms even more strongly this sacramentality, and speaks clearly of 'the sacrament of the diaconate'.[5] To American deacons gathered in Detroit, he said:

> The service of the deacon is the Church's service sacramentalised. Yours is not just one ministry among others, but is truly meant to be, as Paul VI described it, a 'driving force' for the Church's *diakonia*. By your ordination you are configured to Christ in his servant role. You are also meant to be living signs of the servanthood of his Church.

The deacon then is not a super altar server or long-faithful parish helper finally rewarded with a clerical collar or title of 'The Reverend'. He is a sacramental sign, a living icon or image of Jesus Christ. This means that he has a high profile among God's royal, priestly and prophetic people, an official and sacred visibility. He is a public figure, a visible presence, in the name of Jesus himself. As Pope John Paul puts it, 'The Order of the Diaconate can confirm them in the mission they are exercising through a more official consecration and a mandate that is more expressly granted by the authority of the Church by the conferral of a sacrament'.[6]

The distinct identity of the deacon, then, is to be found not in particular tasks he performs, but in his being a sacramental symbol in the midst of the Church. A deacon's ordination changes irrevocably his relationship to the community of the faithful to which he belongs as a fellow disciple.[7] The US Bishops' Committee on the Permanent Diaconate sums up this diaconal distinctiveness:

> The believing community...receives the man as one who, in his sacramental consecration, permanent commitment and specific

ministry, is a sacrament to it of Jesus Christ himself. Ordination is, thus, the sacramental differentiation of a Christian within the community of faith, so that he becomes for it a unique sign and instrument of what Jesus Christ is for the Church and of what the Church must be for the sake of Jesus Christ.[8]

Whatever the deacon is doing, wherever he is – at home, at work, at the altar or at ministry, the deacon is always a deacon. Ordination makes him a public figure, and his privacy has to be seen in a new way. He is recognised by people not only for who he is, but for what he is, an authorised, official minister of Christ and his Church.

This diaconal ministry is nothing new. Though sadly neglected for many centuries, the diaconate is a rich element in the Catholic Tradition. St Athanasius was a young deacon when he exercised great influence at the Council of Nicaea. St Patrick's father was a deacon, as was St Francis of Assisi. Reginald Pole was both deacon and cardinal when he presided at the Council of Trent, a council which wanted to restore the diaconate but which took no practical steps to do so. The Second Vatican Council wanted to and did (*Lumen Gentium*, 29).

A service person in a Servant Church

As *the* sacrament of Christ in the world, the Church itself must be a Deacon Community. The ordained deacon is 'a sacred sign of the character of the Church as a servant' (English and Welsh Bishops).[9] Whatever may be said about the special service of a deacon within the community of faith, this should in no way be seen to undermine or devalue the common and sacred service of that very community, the Church of Christ. Together, as lay people, religious brothers and sisters, ordained ministers, we are the priestly, prophetic and servant People of God. The restored ministry of the ordained deacon is not a rival to the development of lay ministries in the Church, nor to the ancient and continuing service of religious congregations, both of which make visible in all kinds of ways the presence of the Servant Christ in his Servant Church. The deacon's ministry of service can only be properly understood in the context of the sacrament of Holy Orders, a sacrament which serves the 'holy order' of the sacred service of all the baptised.

This sacramental diaconate is many things, but above all it is a service. The US Bishops' Committee speaks of service as 'the deacon's proper mark'.[10] Becoming a deacon is not about seeking status, power or position, or being able to dress up more colourfully on the sanctuary. All ministry of course is service, but the deacon is a servant in a special way.

The deacon is a service person. He is a walking sacrament of Christ the Suffering Servant, a living sign of the Servant Christ and his Servant Church. Pope John Paul teaches that 'the deacon in his degree personifies

Christ the servant of the Father'[11]: at the heart of any diaconal identity and spirituality is the figure of God's servant who brings healing by his wounds and his death (Isaiah 52.13-53.12). Christ the Servant was despised and rejected by his own people, and there is no reason to think that his friends and ministers will be treated otherwise. Any 'glory' that comes with office will be that of the cross of the Easter Jesus. As Pope John Paul remarked, 'Deacons, therefore, are called to participate in the mystery of the cross, to share in the Church's sufferings, to endure the hostility she encounters, in union with Christ the Redeemer'.[12]

The prostration at a deacon's ordination, repeated at the Good Friday liturgy, expresses well the proper spirituality of any minister of Christ. It is to become 'the lowest of the low', and certainly brings us down to earth! It symbolises a person's radical response to Christ's call to serve in some special way.

What kind of service?

The deacon then is a servant, 'imaging' the Servant Christ in his Servant Church. But much the same can be said of both bishop and priest, and of lay ministers. Every deacon served in Christ's name before ordination, anointed and sent forth by Christ through Baptism and Confirmation. So what particular service is the deacon to give? It is in the nature of the diaconate that no clear, precise answer can be given to this question. There is nothing a deacon does which cannot be done by lay people when the circumstances demand. And yet he contributes much simply by the sacred visibility of his lowly service, by his very presence as an ordained minister in the name of Christ and his Church.

Many scholars today question whether the seven men chosen to distribute food in Acts 6 were 'deacons' in our sense of the word, but 'a long tradition has interpreted the episode as the first evidence of the institution of deacons'.[13] Even if this was indeed a key step in the development of the diaconate, the apostles were choosing people to assist them in their ministry, in a way called for by the particular circumstances. St Ignatius reminds us that deacons are 'dispensers of the mysteries of Jesus Christ', 'not deacons of food and drink but officers of the Church of God' (*Trallians*, 2).

The Bishop's Man

By the third century, the deacon was the bishop's right-hand man, helping in whatever way was most useful and fitting. There was an especially close bond between the bishop and his deacons. Wives of deacons may feel rather jealous of one third century description of this bond as 'a single soul dwelling in two bodies' (*Didascalia Apostolorum*, 3.13)! The same document describes one of the deacon's roles as preventing whispering, sleeping, laughing and signalling during the liturgy. Deacons were sometimes referred to as the bishop's eyes and ears, required to 'make all things known to the bishop, even as Christ to the Father' (2.44). They were to keep the bishop informed, as ministers close to the people and yet with 'special access to the episcopal door'.[14]

It is clear that *the deacon was – and is – a helper or assistant*, of the local church and of its leaders. To want to be a deacon is to want to be an assistant – to the bishop and his priests. Archbishop Sepe comments that 'Diaconal ministry is, above all, a service and a help for the episcopacy and the presbyterate. Collaborating with them, the diaconate constitutes a valued service to the Church'.[15] The candidate is asked at his ordination:

> Are you resolved to discharge the office of deacon with humility and love in order to assist the bishop and the priests and to serve the people of Christ?

The *Catechism of the Catholic Church* (n.1554) states that

> Catholic doctrine, expressed in the liturgy, the Magisterium and the constant practice of the Church, recognises that there are two degrees of ministerial participation in the priesthood of Christ: the episcopacy and the presbyterate. The diaconate is intended to help and serve them. For this reason the term *sacerdos* in current usage denotes bishops and priests but not deacons.

The deacon is not the ordinary president of a Christian community and its worship, but assists bishops and priests in their presidency.[16] Sometimes a deacon is given charge of a small community (cf Canon 517.2), but it remains true that it is the bishop and his priests who are ministerial leaders with pastoral authority, while the deacon is a ministerial assistant. As McCaslin and Lawler put it, 'leadership is not a deacon talent but a priest talent'.[17] For the Christian, of course, authoritative presidency itself is always a role of humble service as a 'servant of the servants of God'. Nearly all diaconal presiding is done 'in the absence of a priest', as far as the official documents are concerned. The ministry of a deacon can never adequately substitute for that of a priest. Nor should his ministry undermine or diminish the role of lay people in the Church.[18] One of the deacon's roles is to support and encourage, free and facilitate lay ministers and priests in their own special forms of service. As we shall see, the deacon is a distinctive minister in his own right, neither a lesser priest nor a superior layperson.

A distinctive ministry

The deacon's most visible role is at the side of the bishop or priest at the liturgy, often seen by the people as either a 'mini priest' or an especially dignified species of altar server. Unfortunately some deacons see themselves as the former, and some priests see deacons as the latter, a powerful recipe for confrontation.

But the deacon is neither 'almost a priest' nor 'someone who can do everything a priest can do except consecrate, absolve and anoint'. He has a distinctive ministry of his own, although always as the helper of the one who presides. The roles of priest and deacon are not interchangeable. On the one hand, deacons should not try to be as 'priesty' as possible, sometimes urging for themselves authority to anoint the sick and absolve sinners.[19] The permanent diaconate is not for people who would rather be priests but who become deacons as the next best thing, secretly longing to exchange their dalmatic for a chasuble. On the other hand, priests should not act as though they were deacons. It is extraordinary that there are still places where priests dress up as deacons at Mass in the absence of the 'real thing', even though the Sacred Congregation for Divine Worship stated clearly in a 1972 *Presentation* that '*it is altogether out of place* for a priest vested as a deacon to exercise the deacon's function'.[20] A priest can assist the main celebrant in the absence of a deacon, but he is obliged to wear the liturgical vestments of his own order.[21]

Priests and Deacons

Some priests will respond by saying that they are by ordination deacons as well as priests. This 'layer theory' of ordained ministry bears little relation to the theology of the early Church, and may have helped to undermine the distinctive character of the diaconate. Another theory is that a person moves from the order or college of deacons to the order or college of presbyters at his priestly ordination, and to the order or college of bishops should he be ordained bishop. A bishop is of course a priest, a high priest indeed, but he is not a presbyter, nor is a presbyter a deacon. All three ministries share the one sacrament of orders in varying ways, but this does not have to be seen as climbing the rungs of a ladder or acquiring ever-larger slices of the ministerial pie! Perhaps we are back to the understanding of some early writers, seeing a 'trinitarian' relationship between three really distinct but not separate ministries: the bishop as image of God the Father, with a primacy of origin as the 'source' of the other two orders which share his ministry in different ways.

Unity in diversity

Now that most deacons minister in parishes alongside a priest rather than a bishop, the close bond between a bishop and his college of deacons has largely been lost. Some argue strongly that the Church should re-establish the primacy of the deacon's relationship to the bishop.[22] It is worth noting that the often-quoted statement from Hippolytus that deacons are ordained 'not to the priesthood but for service' actually says in full that 'they are ordained not to the priesthood but *for service to the bishop, to do those things which are delegated to him...*'[23] It may be that each bishop could do more to strengthen the sense of a 'college of deacons' in his diocese.

Whatever can be done to restore the close bond between a bishop and his deacons, such a bond is surely the model for the way priest and deacon should work together, 'a single soul (the spirit of humble service) dwelling in two bodies'. A deacon may well be a helper and assistant, but his ministry complements and enriches that of bishop and priest. In the entrance procession at Mass, the deacon walks alongside the priest – there to assist him but also serving side-by-side with him.

A three-fold ministry

The ministry of the deacon is often divided between the service of altar, word and charity, but in reality all three are intimately interwoven, one service of Christ in his Church. The deacon baptises, assists at marriages, brings viaticum to the dying, officiates at funerals, burials and cremations. Since the fourth century, it is the deacon who solemnly proclaims the Gospel at the Eucharist, not the priest. The Bishops of England and Wales write of the specific teaching role of the deacon, 'the solemn core of which is the proclamation of the Gospel at Mass'.[24] *The General Instruction on the Roman Missal* states:

> By tradition the reading of the extracts from scripture is not a presidential function, but that of an assistant. Hence the deacon – or, *if no deacon is present*, some other priest – should read the Gospel (art. 34)

Whatever the status of the 'seven' in Acts 6, they soon moved on from distributing food to preaching the Good News (Acts 6.8f; 8.4f, 26f). Although scholars disagree about whether or not deacons regularly preached at the Eucharist in the early Church, they do now have a public ministry of evangelisation and catechesis. At his ordination the deacon is presented with the Book of the Gospels and instructed: 'Receive the Gospel of Christ whose herald you now are'. He is to be a Gospel-person, a 'walking Gospel', proclaiming the Good News of Jesus not only in word but by his whole life and ministry. He does this not in isolation, but in partnership with catechists, evangelists and others, helping to build a community which is itself the living Gospel for all to hear.

He is also to be a Eucharistic person, with his own visible role in the celebration but also living out the Eucharist and bringing the presence of Christ into the lives of those he serves. He is to be a man of prayer, praying the Divine Office for the Church and leading the people in intercession to God.

A deacon is sometimes rather like an angel, albeit a visible one. He is a minister who is often simply 'hovering nearby', sometimes unnoticed, perhaps even forgotten or ignored. He will have 'things to do' in the liturgy and elsewhere, but it is his *ministry of presence* which is often most important, simply 'being there' in the name of Christ and with the particular kind of 'sacred visibility' which comes from the sacrament of orders.

The ministry of love and justice

We are used to the liturgical and preaching roles of the deacon. But what of the ministry of 'charity', the ministry of love? Here is a real challenge to every deacon! If you are to represent Christ the Suffering Servant, you must have a special care for the poor and the oppressed. The Church's teaching authority makes it clear that working for justice, peace and human rights lies at the heart of proclaiming the Gospel and of the Church's service of Christ in the world. It also lies therefore at the heart of the deacon's ministry. Archbishop Sepe remarks on the fitting connection between this ministry of charity and the liturgical ministry of the deacon.[25]

In the early Church, the deacon's ministry of charity was clear. He was often responsible for administering care to the poor and needy, sometimes holding sway over the material resources of the Church. Quite a few Roman deacons were elected Pope! It would be easy for the modern deacon to slip into such a role, and there may well be a useful role for deacons to play in the administrative affairs of the diocese, but they have more 'powerful' ways to be of service.

Polycarp described deacons as 'God's and Christ's servants, not people's' (*Philippians*, 5), but we find and serve Christ in the hungry and thirsty, the stranger and the naked, the sick and imprisoned (cf. Matthew 25.31f). There too the deacon will minister to his Lord, and make visible the Church's servant care for God's people. This calls for humble service, a lowly status, often inconvenience, hostility from others, even risk. All true service is open to martyrdom in one way or another, and Christ the Servant teaches us that serving at table and washing feet are sacred actions. Jesus is here among us 'as one who serves' (Luke 22.27; cf. 12.37). If we see such activities as demeaning and 'sub-diaconal', we may well have a sub-Christian notion of service. American Episcopalian deacon Ormonde Plater suggests that after handing over the Book of the Gospels at a deacon's ordination, the bishop should then 'give a large white hand towel to the deacon as a symbol of table-waiting and footwashing'.[26] Pope John Paul encourages deacons 'to take their inspiration from the Gospel incident of the washing of feet', and goes on to remind us that 'the diaconate commits one to following Jesus with this attitude of humble service, which is expressed not only in works of charity, but shapes and embraces one's whole way of thinking and acting'.[27]

Raising the dust

Ormonde Plater gives some interesting thoughts on the roots of the word 'deacon', from the Greek *diakonos*:

> It appears to have descended from the Indo-European roots *dia*, meaning thoroughly, and *ken* or its suffixed o-form *kono*, meaning active. Another possible etymology combines two Greek words meaning 'through the dust', and hence servants may have been 'dusty ones' in the sense of hurried activity on the road.[28]

A deacon then is one called to raise up dust! He is 'one appointed and given grace to be thoroughly active and dusty in the service of the Church and the care of the poor'.[29]

It is tempting to stay put in the ministry of word and altar, dressing in dazzling white alb and richly woven dalmatic. It is safer, more comfortable, less risky. And yet the Word of God we proclaim demands that we work for justice, and the Eucharist we celebrate sends us out to find the Christ we receive in the broken lives of the poor and oppressed, the rejected and the outcast. This may well mean, for example, a special commitment to the homeless and unemployed, to people who have been abused or those with AIDS.

Every deacon therefore must be dedicated to the ministry of charity, of active love, of justice. An understanding of and living commitment to the Church's radical and challenging social teaching should be key qualities required of any candidate for the diaconate, and ongoing formation in this area should be central to any post-ordination programme of study and reflection. Lending his 'sacred visibility' to the Church's work for justice lies at the heart of a deacon's ministry.

Anyone who does work to stir up a Christian community in the realm of social justice always raises plenty of dust. The deacon must be ready to get dirty and dishevelled in the service of Christ in the poor and suffering.

At the Easter Vigil the deacon (not the priest!) lifts high the Paschal Candle amid the smaller ones of the faithful, and sings 'The Light of Christ'. Then he (not the priest!) sings the *Exultet*, proclaiming the great Easter gift of liberation, the breaking of chains, the dispelling of evil. These two diaconal roles sum up much of his whole ministry. The deacon does not of course have a monopoly on service in the Church. He is to lift high the candle of compassion and justice in the midst of God's chosen people, so that all together may bring the light of the Easter Jesus into the darkness of the world.[30]

This ministry is not just Christian social work. It is bringing Christ himself into the lives of the needy, and serving Christ in them. The deacon is a sacramental sign of Christ the Servant 'washing the wounded feet' of humanity.[31] It is a powerfully positive ministry, bearing to others the joy of Christ's selfless love.

Treasure the poor

Real ministry in Christ's name is never easy, especially when it involves disturbing the cosy consciences of others. It is easier to be a false prophet, telling people what they want to hear.

One model for today's deacon is St Lawrence, archdeacon to Pope Sixtus II. He was close to his bishop, and responsible for administering money to the poor. In AD 258 the Emperor Valerian arrested and beheaded the Pope and his deacons. All, that is, except Lawrence, who knew where the Church's 'wealth' was hidden. Lawrence was sent to collect it. Instead he distributed it to the poor, and collected together the blind, widows, orphans, elderly, lepers and lame. 'Here are the true treasures of the Church', he said to the imperial officials. Legend has it that he was tortured to death on a red-hot grid-iron. After a while he asked to be turned over, as he was cooked enough on one side. Lynn Sherman suggests that this was possibly 'the first recorded example of diaconal humour in the face of adversity'.[32] No deacon will survive his ministry without a sense of humour!

The deacon must have as his 'treasure' the Risen Lord who is found not only in the liturgy and the scriptures but also in the lives of those in need. The Church's 'prior option for the poor' must be especially visible – sacredly, sacramentally visible – in the life and ministry of the deacon, as 'walking sacrament' of the Suffering Servant.

The primacy of love

I have given far more attention to the ministry of charity than to the ministries of word and altar.[33] Does the ministry of charity have a primacy over the other two? As Pope John Paul puts it, the three ministries are

> inseparably joined together as one in the service of God's redemptive plan. This is so because the word of God inevitably leads us to the Eucharistic worship of God at the altar; in turn, worship leads us to a new way of living which expresses itself in acts of charity.[34]

In the end, however, love is the heart of the matter, and the ministry of charity has the first call on the deacon in his ministry. The English and Welsh bishops state that 'it is clear that *the first ministry of the deacon is the ministry of charity*'.[35] The American bishops point out that 'from the beginning, and particularly during the first centuries, the diaconate has been *primarily a ministry of love and justice*';[36] this ministry of love and justice aims not only at meeting the immediate needs of people, but also addressing their structural and institutional causes: 'Action on behalf of social justice is thus an integral part of the deacon's ministry of love'.[37] Pope John Paul saw it as a great source of satisfaction that so many deacons in the United States were involved in direct service to the needy.[38]

As Pope Paul VI emphasised, deacons are there to be a 'driving force' for the common service of the whole Church, animating and promoting that service by all. The deacon is ordained for all three ministries, and must be prepared to undertake each of them in some way. Some deacons focus too readily on the ministries of word and altar, and neglect the vital – and essentially diaconal – ministry of charity and of justice. Cardinal Bernardin warns against using deacons for roles which can be carried out by others, and stresses the need to ensure that deacons are left free for their special ministry of charity and justice:

> The fundamental role of the deacon, then, is to perceive the presence of Christ in the needy, the helpless and the poor – and to reveal this presence to the rest of the people of God, including the bishop. Then the deacon's responsibility is to call all of us to respond to that presence – and to do something about it.[39]

A bridge person

In the early Church, the deacon was an intermediary or 'bridge'. He read the signs and passed on the needs and concerns of people to the bishop and priests so that the local church could focus its attention on them. There may still be such a role for deacons in each diocese. In the parish, however, the deacon is an intermediary not so much between priest and people, as between the sacred and the secular, or as Brentwood deacon Ron O'Toole writes, 'the bridge between the sanctuary and the market place'.[40]

Becoming a deacon does not lift a person out of the Christian community. The role of all ordained ministers is to be special servants of the unity of Christ's Church. The deacon is in a special position to help to weave together the living tapestry of the Church. Ordination makes him a particular link in the network of relationships within the Church, with a ministry of bridging, connecting, and harmonising, always intimately united with the many other ministers in the Church, lay and ordained. Far from working in isolation, the deacon has to be involved in true collaborative ministry, partnership in service, rather than simply doing things on behalf of others. As Pope John Paul remarks,

> ... according to the Council the functions assigned to the deacon can in no way diminish the role of lay people called and willing to participate in the apostolate with the hierarchy. On the contrary, the deacon's tasks include that of "promoting and sustaining the apostolic activities of the laity". To the extent that he is present and more involved than the priest in secular environments and structures, he should feel encouraged to foster closeness between ordained ministry and lay activities, in common service to the kingdom of God.[41]

The worlds of work and family

It is often said that the priorities of a married deacon must be – in order – family, job, diaconate. The three are distinct, and the order is right, but they are not separate and cannot be so easily disentangled. The married, employed deacon is a deacon in his family life and in his work, and a key dimension of his distinctive service is precisely his bringing of the sacred, sacramental visibility of his ordained ministry into the intimacy of marriage and the world of work (or lack of work).

The deacon has a special witness to give. Many deacons are in full-time secular employment, and this gives them 'entry into the temporal sphere in a way that is not normally appropriate for other members of the clergy' (Pope John Paul).[42] The Church is often urged to immerse itself more in the world of work, to be there where ordinary people are. The 'worker priest movement' in France emerged from such concerns. The Pope himself calls for the development of a spirituality of work.[43] The deacon is in a special position to carry out a true 'marketplace ministry',[44] a ministry of presence, making Christ and his Church sacramentally there in the midst of daily secular life. The Pope points out that one deeply felt need in deciding to re-establish the permanent diaconate 'was and is that of a greater and more direct presence of Church ministers in the various spheres of the family, work, school, etc...'[45] Much more thought needs to be given to this dimension of the deacon's ministry. We can give so much attention to the many 'churchy' ministries available to the deacon that his distinctive involvement in the secular and the ordinary becomes undermined. In today's society, of course, this involvement may well mean ministry as an unemployed deacon among the unemployed, or later in life as a retired person still involved in ministry. Deacons are in a special position to bring the needs and concerns of those in the marketplace and the dole queue to their local Christian community, its priest and the bishop, but also to bring Christ and his Church to those people with whom he lives and works.

Sacred worship and ordinary life, the Eucharist and service of our neighbour, should never have been put asunder in the first place. As one who moves between the sacred and the secular, the permanent deacon is in a special position to draw them together and bring God's healing and reconciliation.

The deacon brings to God's people the bread of the Eucharist and the bread of practical love, both the presence of Christ himself, the Bread of Life. He proclaims by his ministry that 'what began in the sanctuary continues in the streets', as Ron O'Toole puts it.[46] In his address to the American deacons, Pope John Paul highlighted this dimension of the deacon's ministry:

> This is at the very heart of the diaconate to which you have been called: to be a servant of the mysteries of Christ and, at one and the

same time, to be servant of your brothers and sisters. That these two dimensions are inseparably joined together in one reality shows the important nature of the ministry which is yours by ordination.

The married deacon also brings marriage to the ordained ministry, enriching and complementing the celibate service of the priest. Much more serious reflection needs to be focused on the duality of marriage and ministry in the life together of the deacon and his wife. Both marriage and orders permeate every aspect of the deacon's life: he is always both a husband (and perhaps a father) and an ordained minister. Marriage itself is a servant relationship, signing and ministering God's love to one another, to their children and to others. The American bishops point that that self-giving love is common to the sacraments of marriage and orders, and that there is potential for an integrated spirituality that relates the two sacraments: 'The marriage bond should be enriched by the sacrament of orders, just as public ministry is enriched by married ordained ministers of the Gospel'.[47] Whatever the distinctive way of life chosen by the wife of a deacon (perhaps a distinct ministry apart from her husband's diaconal service, perhaps a kind of team or collaborative ministry with her husband), the continual nurturing and deepening of the mutual self-giving love of husband and wife must always remain the heart of their life together. American deacon Steve Landregan stresses the need to ensure that wives are given the opportunity to grow spiritually with their husbands: 'If not, a chasm may be opened that could endanger both marriage and ministry'.[48] The married deacon is 'a shared person,'[49] but it must always be remembered that he is shared first with his wife, and only then with his work and ministry. Otherwise, we may well end up saying, 'What God has joined together, the diaconate has put asunder'.[50] Truly Christian marriage involves so intimate an intertwining of lives that the married deacon and his wife never minister as *separate* from each other, however *distinct* may be their particular roles and forms of service. Pope John Paul recognised that the response of married deacons was made possible by the love and support and collaboration of their wives.[51] Perhaps this is something which needs to be said more often, by bishops, priests and parish communities.

A ministry of the cross

So what is a deacon, and why do we need him? He is an assistant, a footwasher, a waiter at table, a service person, a hovering angel, a dust raiser, a bridge, all as signs of the Servant Lord in his Servant Church. He will need an 'angelic' quality, prepared often to hover quietly in the background; the patience of a waiter, with many demands on him but with no tips offered; the humility of a footwasher, increasingly important once the dust begins to rise!

Like some deacons in the early Church, there is no reason to think that a deacon's lot today will be an easy one: St Tiburius was reportedly made to walk on burning coals and finally beheaded (AD 288); St Apollonius was sewn in a sack and thrown into the sea (AD 305); St Domitius was stoned to death (AD 362). Some modern-day deacons feel similarly hard done by.

The permanent diaconate is still gradually re-emerging. This does not mean a return to the so-called 'Golden Age' of the diaconate (AD 200-500). We live in a very different world with different needs; as Echlin comments, 'While the services of tomorrow's deacon will be continuous with the ministry of past deacons, they will also be radically different.'[52] It involves what the Taizé community calls 'the dynamic of the provisional', and this can deny the deacon a sense of security and firm identity.

Pope John Paul called on deacons to respect the office of the priest and to cooperate conscientiously with the parish staff, but went on to remind us that 'the deacon also has a right to be accepted and fully recognised by them and by all for what he is: an ordained minister of the word, altar and charity'.[53] The English and Welsh bishops state clearly that 'as an ordained minister of the Church, the deacon is a full member of the parish team, as of right'.[54]

'An important enrichment for the Church's mission'

St Ignatius wrote of deacons as well as of the bishop and his presbyters: 'Nothing can be called a church without these' (*Trallians*, 3). The Church cannot be fully itself without this ministry. McCaslin and Lawler suggest that just as every local church community needs the spiritual leadership of a priest, so also 'it has an essential need for that servant helper called deacon'.[55] Ignatius was referring to the 'local church' of the small urban diocese. Today in many ways the parish priest carries out the role of the bishop in a local parish church, as deputy of the bishop. Can we argue then that there is something vital missing if a parish has no deacon? McCaslin and Lawler continue:

> Outstanding priests and outstanding deacons do not threaten one another, nor are they threatened by outstanding lay people. For, since both are great enablers, they seek out outstanding talent to work side by side with them. A parish, which is the local incarnation of the Church and of Jesus, is not sacramentally whole if it is without either priest or deacon.[56]

This may be to go too far, but we should at least echo Pope John Paul's teaching that in the restoration of the permanent diaconate the Holy Spirit has been mysteriously at work, 'bringing about a new realisation of the complete picture of the hierarchy, traditionally composed of bishops, priests and deacons'.[57] Without the ministry of deacons, that picture is incomplete. The American bishops pointed out that the permanent diaconate was restored out of 'a desire to restore to the Church the full complement of active apostolic ministries'.[58]

None of this makes sense without a keen awareness of the Catholic principle of sacramentality, and a deep consciousness of belonging to a Servant Church, committed to Christ's own ministry of love and of justice. Above all, however, it demands the gift of faith. The diaconate is a response to God's free call and grace, and for people without faith all signs, symbols and sacraments are meaningless. With faith, 'then even a deacon might be something more than he appears to a very casual inspection'.[59] Timothy Shugrue makes an important point about the deacon's ministry and ordained ministry in general:

> Because, as an ordained ministry, diaconate is in the nature of a ritual sign, it has an importance beyond that implied by particular sacred functions entrusted to it... In the Church's glossary of ritual expressions, the ordained deacon is intended to be a word that commands attention, bringing to centre-stage visibility the dimension of 'diaconia' with a new concentration of focus and, indeed, with authority.[60]

This will only be true in the deepest sense if it is the Holy Spirit who animates the deacon's ministry, and if the deacon is a holy man, a man of prayer and a man of love for God and for others – a man of word, altar and charity.

The sacramental grace of the diaconate 'deeply affects the deacon's heart, spurring him to offer, to give his whole self to serving the kingdom of God in the Church'.[61] Whatever the frustrations and sufferings sometimes involved, the diaconate is a great and exalted and joyful ministry, a driving force for the Church's service and a vital gift from God to the Church of today and tomorrow. It makes present in the midst of the Church the joyful, sacrificial and servant love of the Crucified and Risen Lord.

Michael Evans, M. Th
St John's Seminary
Wonersh
Guildford
GU5 0QX

THE TEACHING OF POPE JOHN PAUL II

Address to the Deacons of the United States and their wives

(19 September 1987 – Detroit, Michigan)

Dear Brothers in the service of our Lord,
Dear wives and collaborators of these men ordained to the Permanent Diaconate:

DEACONS: A great and visible sign of the working of the Holy Spirit

I greet you in the love of our Lord Jesus Christ, in whom, as St Paul tells us, God has chosen us, redeemed us and adopted us as his children (cf. Eph 1.3f). Together with St Paul, and together with you today, I praise our heavenly Father for these wonderful gifts of grace.

It is a special joy for me to meet with you because you represent a great and visible sign of the working of the Holy Spirit in the wake of the Second Vatican Council, which provided for the restoration of the permanent diaconate in the Church. The wisdom of that provision is evident in your presence in such numbers today and in the fruitfulness of your ministries. With the whole Church, I give thanks to God for the call you have received and for your generous response. For the majority of you who are married, this response has been made possible by the love and support and collaboration of your wives. It is a great encouragement to know that in the United States over the past two decades almost eight thousand permanent deacons have been ordained for the service of the Gospel.

It is above all the call to service that I wish to celebrate with you today. In speaking of deacons, the Vatican Council said that 'strengthened by sacramental grace, in communion with the bishop and his presbyterate, they serve the People of God in the service of the liturgy, the word, and charity' (*Lumen Gentium*, 29). Reflecting further on this description, my predecessor Paul VI was in agreement with the Council that 'the permanent diaconate should be restored ... as a driving force for the Church's service (*diakonia*) towards the local Christian communities, and as a sign or sacrament of the Lord Jesus himself, who "came not to be served but to serve"' (*Ad Pascendum*, August 15, 1972, Introduction). These words recall the ancient tradition of the Church as expressed by the early Fathers such as Ignatius of Antioch, who says that deacons are 'ministers of the mysteries of Jesus Christ ... ministers of the church of God' (*Trallians*, 2.3). You, dear brothers, belong to the life of the Church that goes back to saintly deacons, like Lawrence, and before him to Stephen and his companions, whom the Acts of the Apostles consider 'deeply spiritual and prudent' (Acts 6.3).

This is at the very heart of the diaconate to which you have been called: to be a servant of the mysteries of Christ and, at one and the same time, to be a servant of your brothers and sisters. That these two dimensions are inseparably joined together in one reality shows the important nature of the ministry which is yours by ordination.

DEACONS: To bring all things into one under the Headship of Christ (Eph 1.3-14)

How are we to understand the mysteries of Christ of which you are ministers? A profound description is given to us by Saint Paul in the reading we heard a few moments ago. The central mystery is this: God the Father's plan of glory to bring all things in the heavens and on earth into one under the headship of Christ, his beloved Son. It is for this that all the baptised are predestined, chosen, redeemed, and sealed with the Holy Spirit. This plan of God is at the centre of our lives and the life of the world.

At the same time, if service to this redemptive plan is the mission of all the baptised, what is the specific dimension of your service as deacons? The Second Vatican Council explains that a sacramental grace conferred through the imposition of hands enables you to carry out your service of the word, the altar and charity with a special effectiveness (cf. *Ad Gentes*, 16). The service of the deacon is the Church's service sacramentalised. Yours is not just one ministry among others, but it is truly meant to be, as Paul VI described it, a 'driving force' for the Church's diakonia. By your ordination you are configured to Christ in his servant role. You are also meant to be living signs of the servanthood of his Church.

DEACONS: A threefold ministry in the service of God's redemptive plan

If we keep in mind the deep spiritual nature of this *diakonia*, then we can better appreciate the interrelation of the three areas of ministry traditionally associated with the diaconate, that is, the ministry of the word, the ministry of the altar, and the ministry of charity. Dependending on the circumstances, one or another of these may receive particular emphasis in an individual deacon's work, but these three ministries are inseparably joined together as one in the service of God's redemptive plan. This is so because the word of God inevitably leads us to the Eucharistic worship of God at the altar; in turn, this worship leads to a new way of living which expresses itself in acts of charity.

This charity is both love of God and love of neighbour. As the First Letter of John teaches us, 'One who has no love for the brother he has seen cannot love the God he has not seen ... whoever loves God must also love his brother' (1 Jn 4.20-21). By the same token, acts of charity which are not rooted in the word of God and in worship cannot bear lasting fruit. 'Apart from me,' Jesus says, 'you can do nothing' (Jn 15.5). The ministry of charity is confirmed on every page of the Gospel; it demands a constant and radical change of heart. We have a forceful example of this in the Gospel of Matthew proclaimed earlier. We are told: 'Offer no resistance to injury.' We are commanded: 'Love your enemies and pray for your persecutors.'

DEACONS: The service of charity is very much needed in the world today

Certainly today's world is not lacking in opportunities for such a ministry, whether in the form of the simplest acts of charity or the most heroic witness to the radical demands of the Gospel. All around us many of our brothers and sisters live in either spiritual or material poverty or both. So many of the world's people are oppressed by injustice and the denial of their fundamental human rights. Still others are troubled or suffer from a loss of faith in God, or are tempted to give up hope.

In the midst of the human condition it is a great source of satisfaction to learn that so many permanent deacons in the United States are involved in direct service to the needy: to the ill, the abused and battered, the young and old, the dying and bereaved, the deaf, blind and disabled, those who have known suffering in their marriages, the homeless, victims of substance abuse, prisoners, refugees, street people, the rural poor, the victims of racial and ethnic discrimination, and many others. As Christ tells us, 'as often as you did it for one of my least brothers, you did it for me' (Mt 25.40).

At the same time, the Second Vatican Council reminds us that the ministry of charity at the service of God's redemptive plan also obliges us to be a positive influence for change in the world in which we live, that is, to be a leaven – to be the soul of human society – so that society may be renewed by Christ and transformed into the family of God (cf. *Gaudium et Spes*, 40f). The 'temporal order' includes marriage and the family, the world of culture, economic and social life, the trades and professions, political institutions, the solidarity of peoples, and issues of justice and peace (cf. *Apostolicam Actuositatem*, 7; *Gaudium et Spes*, 46f). The task is seldom an easy one. The truth about ourselves and the world, revealed in the Gospel, is not always what the world wants to hear. Gospel truth often contradicts commonly accepted thinking, as we see so clearly today with regard to evils such as racism, contraception, abortion and euthanasia – to name just a few.

DEACONS: A special role to play in the world

Taking an active part in society belongs to the baptismal mission of every Christian in accordance with his or her state in life, but the permanent deacon has a special witness to give. The sacramental grace of his ordination is meant to strengthen him and to make his efforts fruitful, even as his secular occupation gives him entry into the temporal sphere in a way that is not normally appropriate for other members of the clergy. At the same time, the fact that he is an ordained minister of the Church brings a special dimension to his efforts in the eyes of those with whom he lives and works.

Equally important is the contribution that a married deacon makes to the transformation of family life. He and his wife, having entered into a communion of life, are called to help and serve each other (cf. *Gaudium et Spes*, 48). So intimate is their partnership and unity in the sacrament of marriage, that the Church fittingly requires the wife's consent before her husband can be ordained a permanent deacon (Canon 1031.2). As the current guidelines for the permanent diaconate in the United States point out, the nurturing and deepening of mutual, sacrificial love between husband and wife constitutes perhaps the most significant involvement of a deacon's wife in her husband's public ministry in the Church. Today, especially, this is no small service.

In particular, the deacon and his wife must be a living example of fidelity and indissolubility in Christian marriage before a world which is in dire need of such signs. By facing in a spirit of faith the challenges of married life and the demands of daily living, they strengthen the family life not only of the Church community but of the whole of society. They also show how the obligations of family, work and ministry can be harmonised in the service of the Church's mission. Deacons and their wives and children can be a great encouragement to all others who are working to promote family life.

Mention must also be made of another kind of family, namely the parish, which is the usual setting in which the vast majority of deacons fulfil the mandate of their ordination 'to help the bishop and his presbyterate'. The parish provides an ecclesial context for your ministry and serves as a reminder that your labours are not carried out in isolation, but in communion with the bishop, his priests and all those who in varying degrees share in the public ministry of the Church. Permanent deacons have an obligation to respect the office of the priest and to cooperate conscientiously and generously with him and with the parish staff. The deacon also has a right to be accepted and fully recognised by them and by all for what he is: an ordained minister of the word, the altar and charity.

DEACONS: In accordance with the Gospel, be servants

Given the dignity and importance of the permanent diaconate, what is expected of you? As Christians we must not be ashamed to speak of the qualities of a servant to which all believers must aspire, and especially deacons, whose ordination rite describes them as 'servants of all'. A deacon must be known for fidelity, integrity and obedience, and so it is that fidelity to Christ, moral integrity and obedience to the bishop must mark your lives, as the ordination makes clear. In that rite the Church also expresses her hopes and expectations for you when she prays:

> Lord, may they excel in every virtue: in love ... concern ... unassuming authority ... self-discipline and in holiness of life. May their conduct exemplify your commandments and lead your people to imitate their purity of life. May they remain strong and steadfast in Christ, giving to the world the witness of a pure conscience. May they ... imitate your Son, who came not to be served but to serve.

Dear brothers, this prayer commits you to lifelong spiritual formation so that you may grow and persevere in rendering a service that is truly edifying to the People of God. You who are wives of permanent deacons, being close collaborators in their ministry, are likewise challenged with them to grow in the knowledge and love of Jesus Christ. And this of course means growth in prayer – personal prayer, family prayer, liturgical prayer.

Since deacons are ministers of the word, the Second Vatican Council invites you to constant reading and diligent study of the Sacred Scriptures, lest – if you are a preacher – you become an empty one for failing to hear the word of God in your heart (cf. *Dei Verbum*, 25). In your lives as deacons you are called to hear and guard and do the word of God, in order to be able to proclaim it worthily. To preach to God's people is an honour that entails a serious preparation and a real commitment to holiness of life.

As ministers of the altar you must be steeped in the spirit of the liturgy, and be convinced above all that it is 'the summit toward which the activity of the Church is directed and at the same time the source from which all her power flows' (cf. *Sacrosanctum Concilium*, 10). You are called to discharge your office with the dignity and reverence befitting the liturgy, which the Council powerfully describes as being 'above all the worship of the divine majesty' (*ibid.*, 33). I join you in thanking all those who devote themselves to your training, both before and after your ordination, through programmes of spiritual, theological and liturgical formation.

DEACONS: Servants of God and friends of Christ

'Sing a new song unto the Lord! Let your song be sung from mountains high!' Sing to him as servants, but also sing as friends of Christ, who has made known to you all that he had heard from the Father. It was not you who chose him, but he who chose you, to go forth and bear fruit – fruit that will last. This you do by loving one another (cf. Jn 15.15f). By the standards of this world, servanthood is despised, but in the wisdom and providence of God it is a mystery through which Christ redeems the world. And you are ministers of that mystery, heralds of that Gospel. You can be sure that one day you will hear the Lord saying to each of you: 'Well done, good and faithful servant, enter into the joy of your Lord' (cf.

Mt 25.21).

Dear brothers and sisters: as one who strives to be 'the servant of the servants of God', I cannot take leave of you until together we turn to Mary, as she continues to proclaim: 'I am the servant of the Lord' (Lk 1.38). And in the example of her servanthood we see the perfect model of our own call to the discipleship of our Lord Jesus Christ and to the service of his Church.

General Audience on 5 October 1993
'Deacons serve the kingdom of God'

These three talks on the diaconate followed a series on the priesthood.[1]

1. In addition to presbyters there is another category of ministers in the Church with specific tasks and charisms, as the Council of Trent recalls when it discusses the sacrament of Orders: 'In the Catholic Church there is a hierarchy established by divine ordinance, which includes bishops, priests and ministers' (DS 1776). The New Testament books already attest to the presence of ministers, 'deacons', who gradually form a distinct category from the 'presbyteri' and 'episcopi'. One need only recall that Paul addressed his greeting to the bishops and ministers of Philippi (cf. Phil 1.1). The First Letter to Timothy lists the qualities that deacons should have, with the recommendation that they be tested before they are entrusted with their functions: they must be dignified and honest, faithful in marriage, and must manage their children and households well, 'holding fast to the mystery of faith with a clear conscience' (cf. 1 Tim 3.8-13).

   The Acts of the Apostles (6.1-6) speak of seven 'ministers' for service at table. Although the question of a sacramental ordination of deacons is not clear from the text, a long tradition has interpreted the episode as the first evidence of the institution of deacons. By the end of the first century or the beginning of the second, the deacon's place, at least in some Churches, is already well established as a rank in the ministerial hierarchy.

2. Important witness is given particularly by St Ignatius of Antioch, according to whom the Christian community lives under the authority of the bishop, surrounded by presbyters and deacons: 'There is only one Eucharist, one body of the Lord, one chalice, one altar, just as there is only one bishop with the college of presbyters and deacons, fellow servants' (*Philad.*, 4.1). In Ignatius' letters deacons are always mentioned as a lower rank in the ministerial hierarchy: a deacon is praised for 'being subject to the bishop as to

---

[1] The text of the three General Audience talks is taken from the English–language editions of *L'Osservatore Romano* for 5, 13 and 20 October 1993. Some of the more detailed references have been omitted from the text as presented here.

the grace of God, and to the presbyter as to the law of Jesus Christ' (*Magnes.*, 2). However, Ignatius underscores the greatness of the deacon's ministry, because he is 'the minister of Jesus Christ who was in the Father's presence before all ages and was revealed at the end times' (*Magnes.*, 6.1). As 'ministers of the mysteries of Jesus Christ', deacons must 'in every way be pleasing to all' (*Trallians*, 2.3). When Ignatius urges Christians to obey the bishop and the priests, he adds: 'Respect the deacons as God's commandments' (*Smyrna*, 8.1).

We find other witnesses in St Polycarp of Smyrna (*Phil.*, 5.2), St Justin (*Apol.*, 1.65.5; 1.67.5), Tertullian (*De Bapt.*, 17.1), St Cyprian (*Epist.* 15 & 16), and later in St Augustine (*De cat. rud.*, I, c. 1,1).

3. In the early centuries the deacon carried out liturgical functions. In the Eucharistic celebration he read or chanted the Epistle and the Gospel; he brought the offerings of the faithful to the celebrant; he distributed communion and brought it to those absent; he was responsible for the orderliness of the ceremonies and at the end dismissed the assembly. In addition, he prepared catechumens for baptism, instructed them and assisted the priest in administering the sacrament. In certain circumstances he himself baptised and preached. He also shared in the administration of ecclesiastical property; he had care of the poor, widows, orphans and helped prisoners.

In Tradition there are witnesses to the distinction between the deacon's functions and those of the priest. For example, St Hippolytus states (second to third century) that the deacon is ordained 'not to the priesthood, but for service to the bishop, to do what he commands' . Actually, according to the Church's mind and practice, the diaconate belongs to the sacrament of Orders, but is not part of the priesthood and does not entail functions proper to priests.

4. With the passage of time, as we know, the presbyterate in the West assumed almost exclusive importance in relation to the diaconate, which in fact was reduced to being merely a step on the way to the priesthood. This is not the place to retrace the historical process and explain the reasons for these changes: it is rather a question of pointing out that, on the basis of ancient teaching, the awareness of the diaconate's importance for the Church became greater and greater in theological and pastoral circles, as did the appropriateness of re-establishing it as an Order and permanent state of life. Pope Pius XII also made reference to this in his address to the Second World Congress of the Lay Apostolate (5 October 1957), when he stated that, although the idea of reintroducing the diaconate as a function distinct from the priesthood was not yet ripe at the time, nevertheless it could become such and that in any case the diaconate was to be put in the context of the hierarchical ministry determined by the most ancient tradition.

The time was ripe at the Second Vatican Council, which considered the proposals of the preceding years and decided on its re-establishment (cf. *Lumen Gentium*, 29). It was Pope Paul VI who later implemented the decision, determining the complete canonical and liturgical discipline for this Order.

5. There were two main reasons for the theologians' proposals and the conciliar and papal decisions. First of all, it was considered fitting that certain charitable services, guaranteed in a stable way by laymen conscious of being called to the Church's Gospel mission, should be concretely expressed in a form recognised by virtue of an official consecration. It was also necessary to provide for the scarcity of priests, as well as to assist them with many responsibilities not directly connected to their pastoral ministry. Some saw the permanent diaconate as a sort of bridge between pastors and the faithful.

Clearly, the Holy Spirit, who has the leading role in the Church's life, was mysteriously working through these reasons connected with historical circumstances and pastoral perspectives, bringing about a new realisation of the complete picture of the hierarchy, traditionally composed of bishops, priests and deacons. Thus a new revitalisation of Christian communities was fostered, making them more like those founded by the Apostles and flourishing in the early centuries, always under the impulse of the Paraclete, as the Acts of the Apostles attest.

6. A deeply felt need in the decision to re-establish the permanent diaconate was and is that of a greater and more direct presence of Church ministers in the various spheres of the family, work, school, etc, in addition to existing pastoral structures. Among other things, the fact explains why the Council, while not totally rejecting the idea of celibacy for deacons, permitted this Order to be conferred on 'mature married men'. It was a prudent, realistic approach, chosen for reasons that can be easily understood by anyone familiar with different people's ages and concrete situations according to the level of maturity reached. For the same reason it was then decided, in applying the Council's decisions, that the diaconate would be conferred on married men under certain conditions: they would be at least 35 years of age and have their wife's consent, be of good character and reputation, and receive an adequate doctrinal and pastoral preparation given either by institutes or priests especially chosen for this purpose.

7. It should be noted, however, that the Council maintained the ideal of a diaconate open to younger men who would devote themselves totally to the Lord, with the commitment of celibacy as well. It is a life of 'evangelical perfection', which can be understood, chosen and loved by generous men who want to serve the kingdom

of God in the world, without entering the priesthood to which they do not feel called, but nevertheless receiving a consecration that guarantees and institutionalises their special service to the Church through the conferral of sacramental grace. These men are not lacking today. Certain provisions were given for them: for ordination to the diaconate they must be at least 25 years of age and receive formation for at least three years in a special institute, 'where they are tested, trained to live a truly evangelical life and prepared to carry out effectively their own specific functions'. These provisions show the importance the Church puts on the diaconate and her desire that this ordination occur after due consideration and on a sound basis. But they are also a sign of the ancient yet ever new ideal of dedicating oneself to the kingdom of God, which the Church takes from the Gospel and raises as a banner particularly before young people in our time too.

General Audience on 13 October 1993

'The deacon has many pastoral functions'

1. The Second Vatican Council determines the place deacons have in the Church's ministerial hierarchy in accordance with the most ancient tradition: 'At a lower level of the hierarchy are to be found deacons, who receive the imposition of hands "not unto priesthood, but unto the ministry". For, strengthened by sacramental grace they are dedicated to the People of God, in conjunction with the bishop and his body of priests, in the service of the liturgy, of the Gospel and of works of charity' (*Lumen Gentium*, 29). The formula 'not unto the priesthood, but unto the ministry' is taken from the text of Hippolytus' *Traditio Apostolica*, but the Council sets it against a broader horizon. In this ancient text, the 'ministry' is specified as 'service to the bishop'; the Council stresses the service to the People of God. Actually, this basic meaning of the deacon's service was asserted at the beginning by St Ignatius of Antioch, who called deacons the 'ministers of God's Church', recommending for this reason that they should be pleasing to everyone (cf. *Trallians*, 2.3). Down the centuries, in addition to being the bishop's helper, the deacon was also considered to be at the service of the Christian community.

2. In order to be allowed to carry out their functions, deacons receive the ministries of lector and acolyte before ordination. The conferral of these two ministries shows the essential twofold orientation of the deacon's functions, as Paul VI explains in his

Apostolic Letter *Ad Pascendum* (1972): 'It is especially fitting that the ministries of lector and acolyte should be entrusted to those who, as candidates for the order of diaconate or priesthood, desire to devote themselves to God and to the Church in a special way. For the Church, which "does not cease to take the bread of life from the table of the word of God and the Body of Christ and offer it to the faithful" considers it to be very opportune that both by study and by gradual exercise of the ministry of the Word and of the Altar candidates for sacred Orders should through intimate contact understand and reflect upon the double aspect of the priestly office'. This orientation is valid not only for the role of priests, but also for that of deacons.

3. It should be kept in mind that before Vatican II the lectorate and acolytate were considered minor Orders. In a letter to a bishop in 252, Pope Cornelius listen the seven ranks in the Church of Rome: priests, deacons, subdeacons, acolytes, exorcists, lectors and porters. In the tradition of the Latin Church three were considered major Orders: priesthood, diaconate and subdiaconate; four were minor Orders: those of acolyte, exorcist, lector and porter. This arrangement of the ecclesiastical structure was due to the needs of Christian communities over the centuries and was determined by the Church's authority.

When the permanent diaconate was re-established this structure was changed and, as to the sacramental framework, was restored to the three Orders of divine institution: the diaconate, presbyterate and episcopate. In fact, in his Apostolic Letter on ministries in the Latin Church (1972), Pope Paul VI suppressed 'tonsure', which marked the entrance into the clerical state, and the subdiaconate, whose functions were given to lectors and acolytes. He kept the lectorate and acolytate; however, they were no longer considered Orders, but ministries conferred by 'installation' rather than by 'ordination'. These ministries must be received by candidates to the diaconate and presbyterate, but are also open to laymen in the Church who want to assume only the responsibilities corresponding to them: the lectorate, as the office of reading the word of God in the liturgical assembly, except for the Gospel, and carrying out certain roles (such as leading the singing and instructing the faithful); and the acolytate, instituted to help the deacon and to minister to the priest (*Ministeria Quaedam*, 5-6).

4. The Second Vatican Council lists the deacon's liturgical and pastoral functions: 'to administer Baptism solemnly, to reserve and distribute the Eucharist, to assist at and bless marriages in the name of the Church, to take Viaticum to the dying, to read Sacred Scripture to the faithful, to administer sacramentals, and to preside at funeral services and burials' (*Lumen Gentium*, 29).

Pope Paul VI in *Sacrum Diaconatus Ordinem* (22,10) laid down in addition that the deacon, 'in the name of the parish priest or bishop, could legitimately lead dispersed Christian communities'. This is a missionary function to be carried out in territories, surroundings, social contexts and groups where a priest is lacking or not easily available. Especially in those places where no priest is available to celebrate the Eucharist, the deacon gathers and leads the community in a celebration of the Word with the distribution of the Sacred Species duly reserved. This is a supply function which the deacon fulfils by ecclesial mandate when it is the case of providing for the shortage of priests. But this substitution, which can never be complete, reminds communities lacking priests of the urgent need to pray for priestly vocations and to do their utmost to encourage them as something good both for the Church and for themselves. The deacon too should foster this prayer.

5. Again, according to the Council the functions assigned to the deacon can in no way diminish the role of lay people called and willing to cooperate in the apostolate with the hierarchy. On the contrary, the deacon's tasks include that of 'promoting and sustaining the apostolic activities of the laity'. To the extent that he is present and more involved than the priest in secular environments and structures, he should feel encouraged to foster closeness between the ordained ministry and lay activities, in common service to the kingdom of God.

The deacon has a charitable function as well, which also entails an appropriate service in the administration of property and in the Church's charitable works. In this area, the function of the deacon is 'on behalf of the hierarchy, to exercise the duties of charity and administration in addition to social work' (Paul VI, *Sacrum Diaconatus Ordinem*, 22.9).

In this regard, the Council makes a recommendation to deacons that stems from the oldest tradition of Christian communities: 'Dedicated to works of charity and functions of administration, deacons should recall the admonition of St Polycarp: "Let them be merciful, and zealous, and let them walk according to the truth of the Lord, who became the servant of all"' (*Lumen Gentium*, 29).

6. Again according to the Council, the diaconate seems of particular value in the young Churches. This is why the Decree *Ad gentes* establishes: 'Wherever it appears opportune to Episcopal Conferences, the diaconate should be restored as a permanent state of life, in accordance with the norms of the Constitution on the Church. It would help those men who carry out the ministry of a deacon – preaching the Word of God as catechists, governing scattered Christian communities in the name of the bishop or parish priest, or exercising charity in the performance of social or charitable works – if they were to be strengthened by the laying on of hands

which has come down from the Apostles. They would be more closely bound to the altar and their ministry would be made more fruitful through the sacramental grace of the diaconate' (*Ad gentes*, 16).

It is known that wherever missionary activity has led to the creation of new Christian communities, catechists often play an essential role. In many places it is they who lead the community, instruct it, and encourage it to pray. The Order of the diaconate can confirm them in the mission they are exercising, through a more official consecration and a mandate that is more expressly granted by the authority of the Church by the conferral of a sacrament. In this sacrament, in addition to a sharing in the grace of Christ the Redeemer poured out in the Church through the Holy Spirit, the source of every apostolate, an indelible character is received which in a special way configures them to Christ, 'who made himself a deacon, that is, the servant of all' (*Catechism of the Catholic Church*, n.1570).

General Audience on 20 October 1993

'Deacons are called to a life of holiness'

1. Among the catechetical topics on the diaconate the one about the spirit of the diaconate is particularly important and attractive, for it concerns and involves all who receive this sacrament in order to carry out its functions in a Gospel perspective. This is the way that leads its ministers to Christian perfection and allows them to give truly effective service (*diaconia*) in the Church, so as 'to build up the Body of Christ' (Eph 4.12).

Here is the source of diaconal spirituality, which is rooted in what the Second Vatican Council calls 'the sacramental grace of the diaconate' (*Ad gentes*, 16). In addition to being a valuable help in carrying out various tasks, it deeply affects the deacon's heart, spurring him to offer, to give his whole self to serving the kingdom of God in the Church. As the very word diaconate' indicates, what characterises the interior mind and will of the one who receives the sacrament is the spirit of service. In the diaconate an effort is made to carry out what Jesus stated about his mission: 'The Son of Man has come not to be served but to serve – to give his life in ransom for many' (Mk 10.45; Mt 20.28).

Doubtless Jesus addressed these words to the Twelve whom he

chose for the priesthood, to make them understand that, although endowed with authority conferred by him, they should act as he did, as servants. The advice applies, then, to all ministers of Christ; however, it has a particular meaning for deacons, for whom the stress is placed explicitly on this service by virtue of their ordination. Although they do not exercise the pastoral authority of priests, in carrying out all their functions their particular aim is to show an intention to serve. If their ministry is consistent with this spirit, they shed greater light on that identifying feature of Christ's face: service. They are not only 'servants of God', but also of their brothers and sisters.

2. This teaching on the spiritual life is of Gospel origin and entered the earliest Christian tradition, as that ancient third century text called the *Didascalia Apostolorum* confirms. In it deacons are encouraged to take their inspiration from the Gospel incident of the washing of feet: 'If the Lord did this', it says, 'then your deacons should not hesitate to do it for the sick and infirm, since you are workers of the truth who have put on Christ' (16.36). The diaconate commits one to following Jesus with this attitude of humble service, which is expressed not only in works of charity, but shapes and embraces one's whole way of thinking and acting.

This perspective explains the condition set by the document *Sacrum Diaconatus Ordinem* for admitting young men to formation as deacons: 'Only those young men should be enrolled to train for the diaconate who have shown a natural inclination for service to the hierarchy and the Christian community' (8). The 'natural inclination' should not be understood in the sense of a simple spontaneity of natural dispositions, however much this too is a presupposition to be considered. It is rather an inclination of nature inspired by grace, with a spirit of service that conforms human behaviour to Christ's. The sacrament of the diaconate develops this inclination: it makes the subject share more closely in Christ's spirit of service and imbues the will with a special grace, so that in all his actions he will be motivated by a new inclination to serve his brothers and sisters.

This service should first of all take the form of helping the bishop and the priest, both in liturgical worship and the apostolate. It scarcely needs remarking here that anyone whose dominant attitude was one of challenging or opposing authority could not properly carry out the functions of a deacon. The diaconate can only be conferred on those who believe in the value of the bishop's and priest's pastoral mission and in the Holy Spirit's assistance guiding them in their actions and their decisions. In particular, it must again be said that the deacon should 'profess reverence and obedience to the bishop' (*ibid.*, 30).

However, the deacon's service is also directed to his own

Christian community and to the whole Church, to which he must foster a deep attachment, because of her mission and divine institution.

3. The Second Vatican Council also speaks of the duties and the obligations that deacons assume by virtue of their own sharing in the mission and grace of the high priesthood: 'while waiting upon the mysteries of Christ and the Church, they should keep themselves free from every vice, should please God and give a good example to all in everything (cf. 1 Tim 3.8-10, 12-13)' (*Lumen Gentium*, 41). Theirs, then, is a duty of witness, which embraces not only their service and apostolate but also their whole life.

In the document *Sacrum Diaconatus Ordinem*, cited above, Paul VI called attention to this responsibility and the obligation it entails: 'Deacons serve the mysteries of Christ and the Church, and must abstain from any vice, strive to please God, and be "ready for any good work" for the service of people. Therefore, because of their reception of this Order, they should far excel others in their liturgical lives, in devotion to prayer, in the divine ministry, in obedience, charity and chastity' (25).

With particular regard to chastity, young men who are ordained deacons commit themselves to observing celibacy and to leading a life of more intense union with Christ. Here too, even those who are older and 'have received ordination ... may not, in accordance with traditional Church discipline, enter into marriage' (*ibid.*, 16).

4. In order to fulfil these obligations and, even more deeply, to respond to the spiritual demands of the diaconate with the help of sacramental grace, the exercises of the spiritual life must be practised, as described in Paul VI's letter; they should: 1) apply themselves to reading carefully and to meditating attentively on the word of God; 2) attend Mass frequently, even daily if possible, receive the Blessed Sacrament of the Eucharist and visit it out of devotion; 3) purify their souls frequently through the sacrament of Penance, having prepared for it worthily through a daily examination of conscience; 4) show a deep, filial love and veneration for the Virgin Mary, the Mother of God (cf. *ibid.*, 26).

Moreover, Paul VI adds: 'It is very fitting for permanent deacons to recite daily at least some part of the Divine Office – to be specified by the Episcopal Conference' (*ibid.*, 27). The Episcopal Conferences are also responsible for establishing more detailed norms for the lives of deacons in accordance with the circumstances of time and place.

Lastly, whoever receives the diaconate is obliged to ongoing doctrinal formation, which continually improves and updates that required before ordination: 'Deacons should not slacken in their studies, particularly of sacred doctrine; they should carefully read the Scriptures; they should devote themselves to ecclesiastical studies in such a way that they can correctly explain Catholic doctrine to others and day by day become better fitted to train and strengthen the souls of the faithful. With this in mind, deacons should be called to regular meetings at which matters concerning their life and sacred ministry will be treated' (*ibid.*, 29).

5. The catechesis I have given on the diaconate, in order to complete the picture of the ecclesiastical hierarchy, thus highlights what is most important in this Order, as in those of the presbyterate and the episcopate: a specific spiritual participation in the priesthood of Christ and the commitment to a life in conformity to him by the action of the Holy Spirit. I cannot conclude without recalling that deacons too, like priests and bishops, who are committed to following Christ in the way of service, share most especially in his redeeming sacrifice, according to the principle Jesus formulated when speaking to the Twelve about the Son of Man, who came 'to serve – to give his life in ransom for many' (Mk 10.45). Deacons, therefore, are called to participate in the mystery of the cross, to share in the Church's sufferings, to endure the hostility she encounters, in union with Christ the Redeemer. It is this painful aspect of the deacon's service that makes it most fruitful.

Selected official and liturgical texts

THE SECOND VATICAN COUNCIL

Article 29 of the Dogmatic Constitution on the Church (*Lumen Gentium*) treats of the ministry of deacon and the restoration of the diaconate as a proper and permanent rank of the hierarchy.[1]

At a lower level of the hierarchy are to be found deacons, who receive the imposition of hands 'not unto the priesthood, but unto the ministry.' For, strengthened by sacramental grace, they are dedicated to the People of God, in conjunction with the bishop and his body of priests, in the service of the liturgy, of the Gospel and of works of charity.

It pertains to the office of a deacon, in so far as it may be assigned to him by the competent authority, to administer Baptism solemnly, to be custodian and distributor of the Eucharist, in the name of the Church to assist at and to bless marriages, to bring Viaticum to the dying, to read the sacred scripture to the faithful, to instruct and exhort the people, to preside over the worship and the prayer of the faithful, to administer sacramentals, and to officiate at funeral and burial services. Dedicated to works of charity and functions of administration, deacons should recall the admonition of St Polycarp: 'Let them be merciful and zealous, and let them walk according to the truth of the Lord, who became the servant of all.'

Since, however, the laws and customs of the Latin Church in force today in many areas render it difficult to fulfil these functions, which are so extremely necessary for the life of the Church, it will be possible in the future to restore the diaconate as a proper and permanent rank of the hierarchy.

But it pertains to the competent local episcopal conferences, of one kind or another, with the approval of the Supreme Pontiff, to decide whether and where it is opportune that such deacons be appointed. Should the Roman Pontiff think fit, it will be possible to confer this diaconal order even upon married men, provided they be of more mature age, and also on suitable young men, for whom, however, the law of celibacy must remain in force.

21 November 1964

---

[1]Translations of this and of Paul VI's *Ad Pascendum* are taken from Austin Flannery (ed.), *Vatican Council II: The Conciliar and Postconciliar Documents* (Costello Publishing Company, Dublin 1975)

POPE PAUL VI: Apostolic Letter, 1972

In 1972, Pope Paul VI issued an Apostolic Letter containing norms for the order of the Diaconate (*Ad Pascendum*). This is the beginning of his letter:

For the nurturing and constant growth of the people of God, Christ the Lord instituted in the Church a variety of ministries, which work for the good of the whole body.

From the apostolic age the diaconate has had a clearly outstanding position among these ministries, and it has always been held in great honour by the Church. Explicit testimony of this is given by the Apostle Paul both in his letter to the Philippians, in which he sends greetings not only to the bishops but also to the deacons, and in a letter to Timothy, in which he illustrates the qualities and virtues that deacons must have in order to be worthy of their ministry.

Later, when the early writers of the Church acclaim the dignity of deacons, they do not fail to extol also the spiritual qualities and virtues that are required for the performance of that ministry, namely, fidelity to Christ, moral integrity, and obedience to the bishop.

St Ignatius of Antioch declares that the office of the deacon is nothing other than 'the ministry of Jesus Christ who was with the Father before all ages and has been manifested in the final time.' He also made the following observation: 'The deacons too, who are ministers of the mysteries of Jesus Christ, should please all in every way; for they are not servants of food and drink, but ministers of the Church of God.'

St Polycarp of Smyrna exhorts deacons to 'be moderate in all things, merciful, diligent, living according to the truth of the Lord, who became the servant of all.' The author of the *Didascalia Apostolorum*, recalling the words of Christ, 'Anyone who wants to be great among you must be your servant', addresses the following fraternal exhortation to deacons: 'Accordingly you deacons also should behave in such a way that, if your ministry obliges you to lay down your lives for a brother, you should do so.... If the Lord of heaven and earth served us and suffered and sustained everything on our behalf, should not this be done for our brothers all the more by us, since we are imitators of him and have ben given the place of Christ?'

Furthermore, when the writers of the first centuries insist on the importance of the ministry of deacons, they give many examples of the manifold important tasks entrusted to them, and clearly show how much authority they held in the Christian communities and how great was their contribution to the apostolate. The deacon is described as 'the bishop's ear, mouth, heart and soul.' The deacon is at the disposal of the bishop in order that he may serve the whole people of God and take care of the sick and the poor; he is correctly and rightly called 'one who shows love for orphans, for the devout and the widowed, one who is fervent in spirit, one who shows love for what is good.' Furthermore, he is entrusted with the mission of taking the holy Eucharist to the sick confined to their homes, of conferring baptism, and of attending to preaching the Word of God in accordance with the express will of the bishop.

Accordingly, the diaconate flourished in a wonderful way in the Church, and at the same time gave an outstanding witness of love for Christ and the brethren through the performance of works of charity, the celebration of sacred rites, and the fulfilment of pastoral duties.

HOMILY FOR THE ORDINATION OF A DEACON

In the Rite of Ordination, a possible homily is provided for the ordaining bishop.[2]

This man, your relative and friend, is now to be raised to the order of deacons. Consider carefully the ministry to which he is to be promoted.

He will draw strength from the gift of the Holy Spirit. He will help the bishop and his body of priests as a minister of the word, of the altar, and of charity. He will make himself a servant of all. As a minister of the altar he will proclaim the Gospel, prepare the sacrifice, and give the Lord's body and blood to the community of believers.

It will also be his duty, at the bishop's discretion, to bring God's word to believer and unbeliever alike, to preside over public prayer, to baptise, to assist at marriages and bless them, to give viaticum to the dying, and to lead the rites of burial. Once he is consecrated by the laying on of hands that comes to us from the apostles and is bound more closely to the altar, he will perform works of charity in the name of the bishop or the pastor. From the way he goes about these duties, may you recognise him as a disciple of Jesus, who came to serve, not to be served.

The bishop then addresses the candidate:

My son, you are being raised to the order of deacons. The Lord has set an example for you to follow.

As a deacon you will serve Jesus Christ, who was known among his disciples as the one who served others. Do the will of God generously. Serve God and humanity in love and joy. Look upon all unchastity and avarice as worship of false gods, for no-one can serve two masters. Like the men the apostles chose for works of charity, you should be a man of good reputation, filled with wisdom and the Holy Spirit. Show before God and humanity that you are above every suspicion of blame, a true minister of Christ and of God's mysteries, a man firmly rooted in faith. Never turn away from the hope which the Gospel offers; now you must not only

---

[2] All texts from the Ordination Rite are in the English translation approved by ICEL

listen to God's word but also preach it. Hold the mystery of faith with a clear conscience. Express in action what you proclaim by word of mouth. Then the people of Christ, brought to life by the Spirit, will be an offering God accepts. Finally, on the last day, when you go to meet the Lord, you will hear him say: "Well done, good and faithful servant, enter into the joy of your Lord."

EXAMINATION OF THE CANDIDATE

At his ordination, the deacon is asked the following questions by his bishop:

Are you willing to be ordained for the Church's ministry by the laying on of hands and the gift of the Holy Spirit?

Are you resolved to discharge the office of deacon with humility and love in order to assist the bishop and the priests and to serve the people of Christ?

Are you resolved to hold the mystery of faith with a clear conscience as the Apostle urges, and to proclaim this faith in word and action as it is taught by the Gospel and the Church's tradition?

Are you resolved to maintain and deepen a spirit of prayer appropriate to your way of life and, in keeping with what is required of you, to celebrate faithfully the liturgy of the hours for the Church and for the whole world?

Are you resolved to shape your way of life always according to the example of Christ, whose body and blood you will give to the people?

Do you promise respect and obedience to me and my successors?

PRAYER OF CONSECRATION

After the laying on of hands, the bishop says the prayer of consecration with his hands extended over the candidate. This is the second part of the prayer:

Lord, look with favour on this servant of yours,
whom we now dedicate to the office of deacon,
to minister at your holy altar.

Lord, send forth upon him the Holy Spirit,
that he may be strengthened
by the gift of your sevenfold grace
to carry out faithfully the work of the ministry.

May he excel in every virtue:
in love that is sincere,
in concern for the sick and the poor,
in unassuming authority.
in self-discipline,
and in holiness of life.

May his conduct exemplify your commandments
and lead your people to imitate his purity of life.
May he remain strong and steadfast in Christ,
giving to the world the witness of a pure conscience.
May he in this life imitate your Son,
who came, not to be served but to serve,
and one day reign with him in heaven.

PRESENTATION OF THE BOOK OF THE GOSPELS

Vested as a deacon, the newly ordained goes to the bishop and kneels before him. The bishop places the Book of the Gospels in the hands of the newly ordained and says:

Receive the Gospel of Christ,
whose herald you now are.

Believe what you read,
teach what you believe,
and practice what you teach.

NOTES FOR INTRODUCTION

[1] General Audience, 5.10.1993.
[2] E.g. Cardinal Bernardin: *'The Call to Service': Pastoral Statement on the Permanent Diaconate for the Archdiocese of Chicago* (1993).
[3] Address published in *Briefing* 6 October 1994 (Vol. 24, no. 19).
[4] The preaching of the homily is indeed reserved to a bishop, priest or deacon, but a layperson can still preach (cf Canons 766-767). The difference is not the function, but the authority shared by the deacon.
[5] General Audiences, 13.10.1993 and 20.10.1993.
[6] General Audience, 13.10.1993; cf the Bishops' Conference of England and Wales *Handbook on the Permanent Diaconate*: 'Being an ordained minister lends authority to the position and work of the deacon'.
[7] This is perhaps the key to understanding the meaning of the 'indelible character' received by the deacon at his ordination.
[8] *Permanent Deacons in the United States: Guidelines on their Formation and Ministry* (US Bishops' Committee on the Permanent Diaconate, 1984 revision) art. 22.
[9] *Handbook on the Permanent Diaconate*, 1987.
[10] *op. cit.* art.25.
[11] Allocution, 16.3.1985, quoted by Archbishop Sepe, *op. cit.* p. 8.
[12] General Audience, 20.10.1993.
[13] Pope John Paul, General Audience, 5.10.1993.
[14] Echlin, *op.cit.* p.168.
[15] *op. cit.* p. 8.
[16] The US bishops state that full leadership over an integral local Christian community is not what a deacon is ordained for (*op. cit.* art.44).
[17] *op.cit.* p.122.
[18] cf. Pope John Paul II, General Audience, 13.10.1993.
[19] Or even to preside at the Eucharist in some places in the early Church.
[20] ICEL, *Documents on the Liturgy* 1963-1979 (Liturgical Press, Collegeville 1982) no. 1372.
[21] *ibid.* no. 1354.
[22] E.g. Timothy Shugrue, *Service Ministry of the Deacon* (U.S. Bishops' Committee on the Permanent Diaconate, 1988) p.31.
[23] *The Apostolic Tradition*, 9.
[24] *Handbook on the Permanent Diaconate*.
[25] *op. cit.* p. 7.
[26] *op.cit.* p.137.
[27] General Audience, 20.10.1993.
[28] *op.cit.* pp.16–17.
[29] *ibid* p.17.

[30] cf. Plater, *op. cit.* p.126.
[31] Echlin, *op. cit.* p.129.
[32] *op. cit.* p.9.
[33] cf Cardinal Bernardin, *op. cit.* p.7: 'We may have done a better job in preparing deacons for their ministries of the word and altar than for carrying out their ministry of charity and social justice'.
[34] Address to the US Deacons in Detroit, 19.9.1987.
[35] *Handbook on the Permanent Diaconate*, 1987.
[36] US Bishops' Committee on the Permanent Diaconate, *op. cit.* art. 6.
[37] *ibid.* art. 38.
[38] Address to US Deacons in Detroit, 19.9.1987.
[39] *op. cit.* p.6.
[40] 'The Diaconate within the Roman Catholic Church' in *The Deacon's Ministry* (ed. Christine Hall; Gracewing, Leominster 1991) p.184.
[41] General Audience, 13.10.1993.
[42] Address to US Deacons in Detroit, 1987.
[43] *Laborem Exercens*, 24f.
[44] Cardinal Bernardin, *op. cit.* p.7.
[45] General Audience, 5.10.1993.
[46] *op. cit.* p.186.
[47] *op. cit.* art. 107.
[48] *Speak Lord!* (US Bishops' Committee on the Permanent Diaconate, 1987) p.42.
[49] Bishops' Conference of England and Wales: *Handbook on the Permanent Diaconate*, 1987.
[50] cf. Steve Landregan, *op. cit.* p.43.
[51] Address to the US Deacons in Detroit, 1987.
[52] *op. cit.* p.127.
[53] Address to the US Deacons in Detroit, 1987.
[54] *Handbook on the Permanent Diaconate*, 1987.
[55] *op. cit.* p.54.
[56] *ibid.* p.63.
[57] General Audience, 5.10.1993.
[58] *Permanent Deacons in the United States: Guidelines on their Formation and Ministry* (US Bishops' Committee on the Permanent Diaconate, 1984 revision) art.19.
[59] Steve Landregan, *op. cit.* p.118.
[60] *Service Ministry of the Deacon* (US Bishops' Committee on the Permanent Diaconate, 1988) pp.25, 27.
[61] Pope John Paul, General Audience, 20.10.1993.